The Sky Embroidered

A book of poems

Bindu Chhibber

BookLeaf Publishing
India | USA | UK

Copyright © Bindu Chhibber
All Rights Reserved.

This book has been self-published with all reasonable efforts taken to make the material error-free by the author. No part of this book shall be used, reproduced in any manner whatsoever without written permission from the author, except in the case of brief quotations embodied in critical articles and reviews.

The Author of this book is solely responsible and liable for its content including but not limited to the views, representations, descriptions, statements, information, opinions, and references ["Content"]. The Content of this book shall not constitute or be construed or deemed to reflect the opinion or expression of the Publisher or Editor. Neither the Publisher nor Editor endorse or approve the Content of this book or guarantee the reliability, accuracy, or completeness of the Content published herein and do not make any representations or warranties of any kind, express or implied, including but not limited to the implied warranties of merchantability, fitness for a particular purpose.

The Publisher and Editor shall not be liable whatsoever...

Made with ❤ on the BookLeaf Publishing Platform
www.bookleafpub.in
www.bookleafpub.com

Dedication

This book is dedicated to my son,, Jayant chhibber, who has walked through fire to be with his mother again. It is because of him my life is in sync and we shall find and make a harmony of our life once more.

To all who have seen heartbreak-

My heart goes out to you.

So does this book!

Preface

If this book finds you, you will find substance that is airy, light and spacious- wistful emotion, raw simplicity and intuitive reflections.

There is immense strength in vulnerability and poetry brings out whatever we assimilate from life. Sunsets, trees and children have been my teachers.

Rain is my first love. I have an ear for music and an eye for the sky.

I could always be found singing despite the circumstances. Dogged by death and disease, I have found strength and serenity.

I attribute it to love- an almost pantheistic devotion to nature, its grace, nobility and resilience. Loss or betrayals hurt us the least, those who are so much in tune with the elements. May our love for the natural in the physical world and faith in human soul sustain us.

As for poetry, poetry is not for someone who demands it to be happy or purposeful. It is what it is, what it wants to be.

We do not write poetry out of a plan. We write poetry because we cannot help writing it. We write when we feel strongly and deeply. That's how we should live- experience wholly, feel strongly and feel good.

Love, hope, despair, loss, disillusionment, disgust are the array of emotions that need to be felt, accepted and expressed. If any of these poignant verses resonate with you, soothe you or offer a cathartic experience, it will be worthwhile.

May we all make the most of our soulful sojourn.

Bindu

Acknowledgements

I deeply acknowledge the blessings of the dear departed family members and the love and affection of all the friends, relatives and students whose prayers have followed and strengthened us in these last few years.

1. The sky embroidered

This book is the sky embroidered just for you
with golden thread and twilight hues.

It is a tree with as many roots hanging from top as those
in earth's womb.

This book is born in the darkness of the serene sea.

It is still a dandelion you may wish upon sweetly.

This book is the substance of clouds that make and
unmake human shapes.

It is a lone traveller in uninhabited wilderness.

This book is the tiny Parjaat, a fragrant offering to the
Gods.

It is an unsuccessful attempt to save all the shades of
green from invading hands.

This book has no community, caste or colour.

It is the chanting of women in a huddle at small temple,
one crying and whispering in Nandi's ear.

This book is a walk in the streets of a sleepy town- a
walk for no purpose but for the sights and sounds.

It is the essence of all the colours of rain.

This book is a friend you don't need to tell your secrets
to because she knows already.

It is love, loss and everything in between.

It is the sigh in music and meaning in the pause.

It is ethereal like all things that refused to die.

It is as brief a visitor as the flame of the forest, the 'Tesu'
that comes dressed just for Holi.

It is the elusiveness of all meaning.

This book is a spatter of dots you cannot connect with
lines.

2. Hold on

Remember, Remember

All the beautiful people you've ever met.

And places that warm your heart.

Remember each bit of love,

Every laughter that rings in your heart

Recall all the innocent pleasures of days past.

Be your own beacon light when the days are dark

Lie low, relax and float.

Make memories your sailboat, my love,

Till the time we reach that happy cove.

3. Between you and me

You seem to me

What I wanted to be,

Doing what I might've done

If I hadn't led down a lonely lane

By the sly usher called circumstance

Chasing butterflies of art

And rainbows to the other world

Are alien to me.

I am mesmerized By monotony.

Not ecstatic enough to rejoice

Not despondent so as to pine.

To you your world, and me mine.

Perhaps you're thinking the same

When you look at me.

Envying me my niche,

My quiet joys in life's high tide.

To all the Lord's lambs

The grass appears to be green

On the other side.

4. Life goes on

Loving you in vain,

Im longing, in pain,

In grieving ,

In despair,

I lived still,

And a beautiful life it was.

5. Sadness

Being happy is an art.

Sadness comes naturally ,

not like the squirrel

that darts in and out of

the mango tree.

It comes like the

stubborn, stray cat

that looks defiantly,

lazing and settling

In the backyard.

Don't challenge her.

Sit with her and breathe.

You'll find the tongue

to tell the stories she tells.

6. Bare

Sometimes

Walking barefoot

Or walking around

With a bare soul

Is good for both-

The soul and sole.

7. Bliss

Come, sit with me

Down on these rocks

Beside the sea.

And let us melt

Like the crimson ball of fire.

Do you feel

The air in the water

And water in the air

That caresses our feet?

Do you feel

The love

That doesn't need a voice

As our hands intertwine?

Let us sigh and

share the stillness,

The sun and sea

and the song that has sprung

up in the backdrop.

Let us count our blessings

In this work weary world.

8. Woman and wings

Every woman

Confined to courtyards

Of pain or disgrace,

Servility or ceremony;

Every woman

Bashed or bullied,

Stifled or scolded,

Leered at or restrained

By blind walls

And treacherous hands;

Every such woman can see

That though she cannot

Yet wing the blues,

The pigeons come down

To pick and peck

At scraps and grains

Of love

Her generous heart scatters.

And when they fly,

They draw her eyes,

Her heart, her lilting laugh

High up and higher

And set the sky on fire.

9. The rescue

I saw the roses ravished by the rain,

Fragrances fading, their blushes jading,

Petals falling prey to pitiless downpour.

Seeing them rushing to a sudden doom,

I snipped them to adorn the vase in my room,

But they sulked and withered before the noon.

Roses were ravished by the rain,

I thought of saving them the pain,

Ah foolish hope. Ah petty pride!

How you have proved me wrong again!

10. Therapy

Cooking is therapeutic.

So is washing , ironing

And gardening too.

Have you ever wondered

Why do all the women need so much therapy?

11. Go gently

Part if you wish

Part if you will

But let it not be rough

Like ripping of wood

Or scraping the flesh.

Go if you know

You want to go

Naturally,

Gently,

Like a

Babbling brook

Divides or multiplies

Behind a Lantana shrub,

Two streams

Flowing

Twinkling

Merrily

At each other

As they drift

And flow

Farther away.

12. Metamorphosis

Hate-

You give some,

You get some.

What you get becomes your story,

One that you constantly

enjoy, embellish and share,

until the grudge

hardens like plaque

in your veins.

And seething with anger

rising up

In the throat like phlegm,

your eyes turn cold.

Mark the moment.

If you glance

in the mirror

You'll see that

slowly,

inadvertently

you are turning into

the one you hate.

13. Loss

Hold each your own, for I know how,

It hurts when love you lose,

Each dreary moment bruised with grief,

Each hour tinged with blues.

How each day ends in endless grief,

Each month dry sorrow reaps,

And how each painful passing year,

Casts backward glance and weeps.

14. Mothers

Ties snap soundlessly.

The umbilical cord goes first.

Then mother's pallu

That the toddler had

Held and followed.

The apron strings go next,

Ridiculed.

And the mother

Who fed her kids

Endlessly from the

Bottomless skillet

Of her overflowing heart

Surrenders to seclusion.

But for the intermittent

Barbs of her son's wife-

That the son was spoilt rotten

By her unbridled love,

That the pickles she makes

Are harmful as poison,

That the two cookies

She impulsively ate

Had come from an

Expensive bakery.

That the old should be

silent, dignified or dead.

If there were no mothers,

Who would we blame

For our failures,

Debts, sour relations,

And the misery

We have made of our lives?

15. Shadows

On the terrace

Beneath the shade

Of neighbouring Neem,

The dog plays hide-and-seek

With his shadow.

And I, with mine.

16. Lifeline

I look at a tree, mesmerized.

If only I could walk into it,

Step into its shoes

I mean, roots.

An IV stuck in my

Outstretched arms,

Green blood pulsing

Through my veins,

I sway to the symphony

Of the balmy breeze.

Forever rooted,

Forever free.

17. Happiness

Happiness is not in answering

" I am not unhappy!"

Happiness is not in questioning

" Am I happy?"

Happiness is in freedom

Happiness is in acceptance-

In surrendering

to the wholeness

of experience.

And crying out

in sheer joy

at the beauty of it all.

18. Quarantine

Already buried

In our tomb-like homes,

We still fear death.

Allowing life to pass us by,

Waiting,

With bated breath.

19. Closure

When I left the door open,

Waited and wilted,

You demurred and drifted.

My heart is closed now.

Do not knock.

All is quiet and still.

20. Winter

Season of rustling silks

Soft sun and silent snow,

Of cosy fires, of quilts

And sweet desserts, you know.

Can you espy

What warmth doth lie

In sulky Winter's heart?

For all he does

Is kill with chill

Come, wink

Sneer and depart.

21. Definition

I am defined by

How fair I am,

How round is the roti I make,

And how much my father

Can spend at the wedding.

You are defined too,

By How much you earn

At that (preferably government) job

And an impressive list

Of your ancestral property.

Our parents are defined

By their sustained slogging

And dogged determination

To arrange an ideal life for us.

Together we shall pay off their dues.

Now you shall define this as feminist poetry.

22. Flowers lament

Flowers rue their fate,

Cruelly plucked to decorate

Idols - clay or flesh.

23. Siesta

I see the old man

enjoy his siesta

on a hard boulder

beside the naalah,

His right hand

across his eyes,

a shield from the

cruel Madras noonlight,

Tamil songs blaring

on a transistor

perched over his lungi.

His sweet dreams mock Insomnia.

24. Blue

All my life I lived

As if I owned a blue Porsche.

When all I had was the blue above

And the blue beneath my feet, I think

As I stand entranced

In the shifting, tickling sand

Of a summer beach.

25. Death

Death from afar

is news

we read sparingly,

And sometimes offer

A sigh as tribute.

Death from a distance

known is a story

we share interspersed with

'If only' ' Perhaps' or 'karma'.

But when it creeps

And strikes home up close,

It is just Death-

Pure, dark and stark,

And takes all thought off

the crazed mind

and wind out of your lungs,

until you are a zombie

without purpose or pain.

26. Safekeeping

Things kept carefully

Somewhere in a safe corner

Are difficult to find.

(Haiku)

27. Enchanted

I do have promises to keep,

And miles to go before I sleep.

But breezes make the boughs sing

The butterfly flaunts a rainbow wing

How buds and fragrant flowers abound

As frail clouds peer over the ground

And when I saw the cactus bloom,

I fell into a wondrous swoon.

28. Elusive love

The pixie cloud does a half sashay
Around the sleepy moon.
The moon sighs at the setting sun
Oh why He leaves so soon.

The sun looks wistful
At the sensual color- spattered shore
The shore has one eye on the tide
Wishing she'd love him more.

The tide is high when she's with
the breeze so heady their love.
But the breeze would hardly stop or stay.
His eyes are known to rove.

So when he says he loves me to
the moon and back I smile,
Love is elusive, hard to hold
but let's love in this while.

29. Let go

In the tug of war of life,

I pulled for years in vain.

And when I let go suddenly,

With a crash, demons were slain.

30. Spring fervour

It is bedlam

up on the terrace.

The land adjacent

to my house

has all the makings

of a noisy spring.

The moringa tree

Is bowed with flowers

fragrant, fragile

easy to fall

as if they already

know of their

miracle powers

newly discovered

By seekers of health .

And nearby the lush

mango tree is blooming too

And though the blossoms

have little beauty or aroma,

they still hold a promise

of delicious sweetness

in the days to come.

The squirrels

The bulbul

The koel

parrots and pigeons

and the tiniest black bird

all clamour for attention

and food.

The Neem looks leafless

quite bare and withered too.

But holds no desolate air

because Trees know

not to search a reason

It's all for a season.

Soon here and there

fresh shoots of green

erupt unseen

until the tree

is an explosion of

rich, lush green.

Even now, see how

one squirrel

and the Indian robin

prefer the perch

of the spacious Neem.

One bird is enough

of an orchestra

in an afternoon.

31. Weeping beauty

Flush out all sense

And nonsense

With a good cry.

Shake all the heaviness off you.

Enjoy the post-cry peace.

Why just the beauty sleep,

Once in a while

One needs a beauty weep.

32. Phantasm

The memory

The pain

The never-again

The longing

The words

That magic touch

The fun

The winter sun

The warming glance

The romance

Was any of it real

Or the child of a reverie

On a breezy rainy afternoon?

33. The wall

She was so cheerful

And at ease

On her own.

Why did she have to

Keep breaking her head

Against that heartless wall?

Perhaps it was the paint,

All six foot high,

The security,

The rugged coating,

The cracks sprouting

Tender weeds.

Or that her children

Often sat leaning

Against it?

Her forehead bled,

And eyes swelled

Till every dream

And desire oozed out

Bit by bit.

She wished to escape

When the scowling wall

Came crashing down on her.

They say her husband

Cried the most at her cremation.

34. All the same

Everyone is a foreigner somewhere

Every boundary is a child of fear

Every heart is a clamorous battlefield

Every sleep is a coming of newborn hope

Every star is a moment of love frozen in time

Every day is a passage through woods unseen

Every smile is an angel passing through someone's face.

Everyone who lives by the labour of his hand is an
epitome of grace.

35. Bindu

Sit quietly, he said.
Focus on
The divine light
In your heart.
'Demigods with booming
Voices teach us silence
And stillness. Amazing art!'
I scoffed. I fidgeted .
But did as I was told.
Out came tumbling
From the forgotten attic,
Darkness
Desires
Misery
Malice
Songs unsung,
Tales untold,
Friends unmade,
Crimes undiscovered,
All the fears locked away,

All the guilt of living on,
So it went on & on
Furtive streams of salt escaped
Down my stricken face.
Until he told me
I was nothing but
Part of an unseen whole.
All the stories I'd told myself
Were dreams woven
Within a dream.
Then I rested on the tiny speck
A point, a dot in the vast universe
The Bindu, that is nothing
That is me.

www.ingramcontent.com/pod-product-compliance
Lightning Source LLC
LaVergne TN
LVHW021234200726

843509LV00012B/1484